EUROPA ⚔ MILITARIA № 14

RED ARMY UNIFORMS OF WORLD WAR II

IN COLOUR PHOTOGRAPHS

ANTON SHALITO & ILYA SAVCHENKOV

**Introduction and captions by
ANDREW MOLLO**

**Photography by
ALEXANDER KOZLOV & IGOR PYSKARYOV**

Windrow & Greene

This edition published in Great Britian by
Windrow & Greene Ltd.
5 Gerrard Street
London W 1V 7LJ

Reprinted 1995

Author's note

Several years ago we and some of our friends became interested in the uniforms and equipment of the wartime Red Army - a subject which at the time had few devotees. While collecting the objects we began to focus attention on recreating the look of the Red Army as recorded in old newsreels and photographs. Alongside the uniforms and equipment we also began to save old photographs, paintings, military books, ephemera such as newspapers, postcards, photograph records, busts of our former leaders - even old motor vehicles. We now also undertake various research projects and conduct archaeological digs. With this book we introduce ourselves to an international readership in the hope that this, our first effort, will not be too harshly judged, and that our reconstructions will bring colour and detail to a subject hitherto shrouded in black and white.

Anton Shalito
Ilya Savchenkov
Moscow 1992

Acknowledgements
Uniforms modelled by Ilya Savchenkov, Anton and Tanya Shalito, Sergey Savin, Kirill Cyplenkov and Maxim Boxer. Russian captions translated by Alexey Soloviev. Thanks also to Gerard Gorokhoff for his help and advice.

A CIP catalogue record for this book is available from the British Library

ISBN 1-872004-59-8

INTRODUCTION

The period covered by the photographic reconstructions in this book - 1935 to 1945 - includes two of the three most important changes which took place during the development of the uniforms of the Red (from 1946, Soviet) Army. During the revolutionary phase and until the end of the 1920s the disruption to industry meant that the armed forces had to rely on whatever happened to be available - which were the uniforms of the former Tsarist army, albeit stripped of Imperial emblems and badges of rank. To these were added quite considerable stocks left behind by the Allied intervention forces when they departed at the end of the Russian Civil War (1919-1922).

Ironically, the uniform that came to epitomise the Red Army soldier - the long buttonless greatcoat with coloured tabs across the front, and the pointed cloth helmet - were also found in Tsarist stores. They had been designed and manufactured in quantity in 1913 as part of the celebrations of the 300th Jubilee of the House of Romanov.

Throughout the late 1920s and early 1930s the Soviet government struggled with the problem faced by all revolutionary regimes which have tried to build a revolutionary army out of the ruins of an old conservative one. Among the first decrees issued by the Revolutionary Council was the abolition of all military and civil ranks, privileges and honours. This was not difficult; but replacing them was. How was a new, effective, disciplined army to be created without a hierarchy identifiable by its uniforms and insignia? By 1935 the experiment had come to an end, and that December officers - but not generals - were restored their traditional titles and more military-looking uniforms. These included distinctive uniforms for the air and tank arms; due to their technical nature both of these enjoyed much greater prestige and propaganda value, in a society ostentatiously forcing through a crash industrial modernisation programme, than the still predominently horse-drawn and foot-slogging conventional mass.

On 7 May 1940 the restoration of rank titles was completed; "commanders" were now generals once more, and "platoon" and "section" commanders, sergeants. With the titles many of the other trappings of the still much-maligned Tsarist army also returned. Parade and undress uniforms for general officers were piped with scarlet; their breeches and trousers acquired wide scarlet stripes, and their headdress a cockade. All these changes, together with those more practical innovations necessitated by the shortcomings shown up by the Winter War against Finland in 1939-40, were percolating through the Soviet empire when the Germans struck on 22 June 1941.

The reintroduction of military rank titles and prestige from the mid-1930s coincided with the most ruthless political purge of the upper echelons of the Red Army, robbing it of many of the experienced old Bolsheviks and the most promising younger commanders alike. Most of those who survived were trusted only by Stalin; the army was demoralised, its officers personally cowed and professionally inert.

The devastation and chaos caused by the Axis attack, coupled with incompetence, refusal to take individual responsibility for command decisions, and the unwieldy system of dual control by military commander and party commissar, led to the loss of most of the air force and the encirclement and destruction of whole armies. Despite these successes the Germans failed to take either Moscow or St.Petersburg.

In an effort to improve military competence and restore morale, Stalin abolished dual control and subordinated the commissar to the military commander. In May 1942 formations which distinguished themselves were awarded "Guards" status and special colours, while their personnel received increased pay and a special breast badge.

But these concessions to the military pride of a demoralised army were nothing compared to the most radical decision taken by the Supreme Soviet, after bitter debate, during the dark days of 1942. *Prikaz 25* of the Commissar of Defence, dated 15 January 1943, restored the traditional shoulder-boards to the Russian soldier. This apparently fairly trivial point of uniform design had great historical resonance in Russia. From the very first days of the Revolution, throughout the Civil War and until January 1943, shoulder boards or *pogoni* were the very symbol of Imperial tyranny. During the Revolution and Civil War an officer caught wearing *pogoni* risked having the stars of his rank replaced by long nails driven through the lace into his shoulders; yet now, suddenly, they were restored, as part of a conscious propaganda programme to enlist every symbol and instinct of traditional Russian patriotism in the defence of the Motherland. It is said that the first *pogoni* were made from stocks of original lace left over from before the Revolution. At the same time the tunic and blouse were restored to their pre-Revolutionary cut.

The change-over to the new uniforms was, of course, gradual, and it was not uncommon to see *pogoni* being worn on uniforms that had not yet been stripped of the old collar patches. Despite these changes there remained something distinctly "Soviet" in the look of the Red Army officer and soldier. The peaked cap retained its

"Japanese" style, the tunics and greatcoats seemed to have exaggeratedly wide shoulders, and the boots continued to be worn low on the calves. Whilst the Red Army man at the end of the war projected a powerful, no-nonsense image, elegance had yet to be achieved.

On 21 June 1945 the great Victory Parade was held in Moscow to celebrate the crushing of Hitler's Germany - a victory to which the Red Army had made by far the greatest contribution, at the greatest cost in men and materiel, of any of the Allied armed forces. Its commander, Marshal of the Soviet Union Zhukov, and his fellow marshals and generals appeared in a uniform introduced specially for the occasion. The colour of this uniform was officially designated "wave green"; however, this colour had first appeared in the army as "Tsar's green" in 1910. Officers and men wore a single-breasted tunic or *mundir,* which had already made an appearance in 1940, when it began to be introduced as a standard item before the outbreak of war put an end to its issue.

Thus it can be seen that the uniform of the Red Army gradually reverted to that of the pre-revolutionary Tsarist army, with the exception of the Soviet emblem that appeared on the headdress and on some insignia. In 1975 the final uniform of the Soviet Army was introduced; but today this would require only minimal change for it to become the first uniform of the new Russian Army.

*   *   *

Unfortunately, although this book represents an unprecedented colour reference to original wartime uniforms, it has not been possible to illustrate examples of all variations of the clothing worn by the Red Army and Navy during the Great Patriotic War; and I would like to explain why.

At the end of the war demobilised soldiers returned home wearing their uniforms, albeit stripped of their badges of rank; indeed, these post-war years were known as "the greatcoat period", because the man in the street usually wore his old military greatcoat for lack of anything better. (Even today it is not unknown for an elderly veteran to wear his wartime officer's tunic, without the shoulder boards, as street dress.) All types of special clothing and equipment, such as the steel helmet, tank and flying helmets, overalls of various sorts, camouflage uniforms and flying clothing were taken back into store, with only a few examples remaining in private hands. Those items worth keeping were stored for re-issue; the rest were destroyed.

When I started collecting in the 1970s there was little interest in the subject, and the few items that appeared on the market were usually quite cheap. One of the best places to find Red Army items was Vienna, where it seemed that the Soviets had left much behind when they withdrew from Austria in 1955. Austrian firms had been quick to switch from making caps, uniforms and insignia for the forces of the Greater German Reich, and began to satisfy the needs of the Red Army. It is curious to see German uniform materials used in the manufacture of Soviet shoulder boards, and the backs of Soviet buttons stamped with the letters RZM (Reichszeugmeisterei). Neither did East German firms waste time: I have seen Red Army caps made by Robert Lubstein in Berlin, and officers' belts stamped with a Dresden maker's name and dated 1947.

Since the end of the war the Soviet film industry has made literally hundreds of war films, all of which required an enormous number of uniforms. Most of the field uniforms and equipment, and the men to wear them, were provided by the Armed Forces; but uniforms required by actors playing the roles of well-known Soviet personalities were specially made, from the same materials and by the same tailors as the originals, so today it is virtually impossible to tell one from the other. Sadly, many of the original uniforms that found their way into the studios after the war have been used so often that few remain, and those that do have been altered so many times that they are of little interest. Many items finding their way into private collections these days bear the inventory numbers and stamps of Lenfilm and Mosfilm studios.

In 1975 I was able to inspect the reserve collection of the Central Museum of the Soviet Army in Moscow. There were rows of uniforms belonging to Stalin and his marshals and generals - but not a single example of a common soldier's uniform. It is both ironic and sad that a museum dedicated to the glory of the Red Army of Workers and Peasants should have attached so much importance to the cult of the personality, and so little to the ordinary soldiers whose almost superhuman endurance and self-sacrifice brought about the defeat of Nazism.

The Red Army is the last of the great combatant armies of World War II to have its "look" recreated in colour photographs, and I am sure that those who are interested in this subject will find in this book the answers to many of their questions, and inspiration for their hobby, be it modelling, painting, re-enactment or collecting. There is no doubt in my mind that the uniforms and equipment of the Red Army have hitherto been underrated in the West from the point of view of colour, design and variety; and that the scarcity of certain types of material will underwrite its value and guarantee its collectability.

Andrew Mollo
London
May 1993

RED ARMY RANKS 1935-45

3 Dec.1935	7 May 1940	15 Jan.1943	27 Oct.1943
Marshal of Soviet Union	Marshal of Soviet Union	Marshal of Soviet Union	Marshal of Soviet Union
Komandarm. 1st Rank	–	–	Senior Marshal of Arty.etc **(1)**
			Marshal of Arty. etc
Komandarm. 2nd Rank	General of the Army	General of the Army	General of the Army
Komcor.	Colonel-General	Colonel-General	Colonel-General
Komdiv.	Lieutenant-General	Lieutenant-General	Lieutenant-General
Kombrig.	Major-General	Major-General	Major-General
Colonel	Colonel	Colonel	Colonel
–	–	Lieutenant-Colonel **(2)**	Lieutenant-Colonel
Major	Major	Major	Major
Captain	Captain	Captain	Captain
Sen.Lieut.	Sen.Lieut.	Sen.Lieut.	Sen.Lieut.
Lieutenant	Lieutenant	Lieutenant	Lieutenant
–	Jun.Lieut.	Jun.Lieut.	Jun.Lieut.
Sgt.Major **(3)**	Sgt.Major	Sgt.Major	Sgt.Major
–	Sen.Sergeant	Sen.Sergeant	Sen.Sergeant
Platoon Commander	Sergeant	Sergeant	Sergeant
Section Commander	Jun.Sergeant	Jun.Sergeant.	Jun.Sergeant
Yefreitor **(4)**	Yefreitor	Yefreitor	Yefreitor
Red Army Man	Red Army Man	Red Army Man	Red Army Man

Notes:
(1) The ranks of Senior Marshal of Artillery, Aviation and Tanks were introduced on 4 February 1943.
(2) The rank of Lieutenant-Colonel was introduced on 26 July 1940.
(3) The Russian title for this rank is Starshina.
(4) From German, Gefreiter, meaning a soldier freed from menial duties; in many armies designated as Private First Class.

SELECT BIBLIOGRAPHY

Chief of the General Staff, *Uniforms and Insignia of the Soviet Army and Para-Military Forces*. Army HQ, Ottawa, 1950

Chrestiel, G.H., *Types et Uniformes de l'Armée Rouge vus à Berlin en 1945*. Editions du Panache, Paris, 1946

Die Rotearmee (Fremde Heere im Bild V). Ludwig Voggenreiter Verlag, Potsdam, 1935

Haritonov, O.V., *Uniforms and Marks of Distinction of the Soviet Army 1918-1958*. Artillery Historical Museum, Leningrad, 1960

Herfurth, D., *Militärische Auszeichnungen der UdSSR*. Militar-Verlag der DDR, Berlin, 1987

Ivanow, U.N., *Kurze Zusammenstellung über die Russische Armee*. Verlag R.Eisenschmidt, Berlin, 1929

Korneev, A.F. & Pastukov, I.P. (consul.), *The Nation's Sidearms* (catalogue of collection of Central Order of the Red Banner, Museum of the Armed Forces of the SSR). Moscow, 1978

New Notes on the Red Army, No.2: Uniforms and Insignia. War Office, London, Oct.1944

Putnikov, G., *Orders and Medals of the USSR*. Novosti, Moscow, 1990

Taschenbuch Russisches Heer. Bestimmt für den Gebrauch der Truppe im Felde vom 15.4.43 Ic Unterlagen Ost, Merkblatt 19/1 (Anhang 2 zu H.Dv.1a, Seite 19 1fd.Nr.1)

The Soviet Army: Uniforms and Insignia. War Ofice, London, Aug.1950

Zaloga, S.J., *Soviet Army Uniforms in World War 2* (Uniforms Illustrated No.8). Arms & Armour Press, London, 1985

Zaloga, S.J., *The Red Army of the Great Patriotic War, 1941-45* (Men at Arms No.216). Osprey Publishing, London, 1989

Lieutenant of Artillery, service dress, 1940

This junior officer wears the "everyday" or service uniform as laid down by *Prikaz 176* of 3 December 1935. His service cap has the black band and scarlet piping of his arm of service. The tunic is the so-called "French", characterised by the four pockets and the piping in arm-of-service colour at collar, front closure and cuffs.

His rank insignia are of the sequence introduced in 1936, and are displayed on collar and forearms. The collar patches are in Artillery black, edged with officer's gold braid, and bear the Artillery's crossed cannons above the two red-enamelled, gold-edged squares of Lieutenant's rank. The sleeve chevrons - two red and two gold alternating - also indicate the exact rank.

He wears dark blue *sharovari* semi-breeches with scarlet Artillery piping; the ankle boots and knee-length gaiters are an optional alternative to the traditional kneeboots. Note the Sam Browne belt with cut-out Soviet star buckle; and on his left breast the Order of the Red Star, instituted in 1930.

Lieutenant-General of Rifle Forces, summer undress uniform, 1940

The Red Army referred to their infantry branch as Rifles for traditional reasons: the term for riflemen - *streltsi* - carried greater historical prestige than that for infantry - *pyekhoty*.

This white undress summer uniform for general officers was introduced in July 1940. The white peaked cap was made in one piece, but there was also a white cover which fitted over the crown of the normal khaki-topped service cap. Note the general officers' new circular cockade cap badge, and double gold cords. The general officer's cap band and collar patches were in red for Rifles and those on the general list; Tank, Artillery and Engineer generals wore black. Only General of the Army and above wore red irrespective of their former arm. The sleeve rank insignia for all general officer ranks below General of the Army differed only in the size of the separate embroidered star; the broad gold lace chevron thinly edged at the bottom with red was worn by all grades. General of the Army had an additional broader red edging at the top of the chevron.

Sergeant of Rifle Forces, service uniform, 1940

This sergeant lining the route during a parade in Moscow's Red Square wears the standard summer uniform of the Red Army rank and file in accordance with 1935 regulations. The traditional blouse or *gymnastiorka*, at this date with a fall collar, is in summer weight and shade; note the difference in colour between it and the *sharovari*. The plain pockets are typical of the rank and file. His collar patches are in Rifles colours, crimson piped with black, with a triangular brass device in the upper corner, and the three red-enamelled triangles in front of the badge of arm identifying the exact rank.

He wears the 1916 pattern French Adrian helmet with, on the front, a thin brass five-point star sprayed red except for the hammer and sickle device and the edges. Although gradually replaced by the 1936 pattern, the Adrian helmet continued to appear at May Day parades until 1941. His leather boots are of the traditional calf length. He holds the standard issue M1891/30 Mosin Nagant rifle, with socket bayonet fixed, and has a full set of leather equipment.

On the left breast he displays the badge of a "Voroshilov Marksman", of which literally millions, in various categories, were awarded to members of the "Osoaviakhim" voluntary organisation.

Junior Sergeant of Artillery, winter field dress, 1940

The winter uniform which was theoretically standard throughout the Red Army well into the first year of the Great Patriotic War. The cloth helmet - the *shlem* - bears a cloth star in Artillery black behind the enamelled Red Army star badge. The great-coat bears Artillery collar patches in black piped with scarlet, with brass cannons above the enamelled triangle of this rank. Some equipment was still manufactured in leather, though canvas was increasingly substituted from the late 1930s. This soldier has a leather belt and ammunition pouches, and leather-reinforced canvas suspenders for the M1938 field pack introduced in 1939. The broad canvas sling is that of the BN gasmask bag. His weapon is the M1891/38 carbine.

Junior Sergeant of Artillery, winter field dress, 1940

This rear view of the figure on page 9 shows a typical arrangement of personal equipment. The pack is the lightweight M1938 introduced the following year, of olive canvas trimmed with leather. It has two external pockets for toilet gear and rifle accessories, and accomodated spare under-wear and the cape/shelter half when the latter was not stowed externally. It has straps underneath for attaching tenting gear; and a separate ration pouch was often strapped beneath the pack (if available - it was in short supply from 1941). The greatcoat and/or - as here - the cape/shelter half could be stowed strapped to the top and sides of the pack. The shelter half or *plashch-palatka* was of olive fabric and had a drawstring hood. One of a number of different aluminium mess tins and pots hangs from the pack. Strapped to the belt on the left hip is the entrenching tool in its canvas pouch; it is identical to the Tsarist pattern, and both head and wooden handle were often painted olive green. Slung on the right hip is the BN gasmask in its carrying bag.

Red Army Man, Rifle Forces, winter field dress, 1940

This slightly contrasting rear view of an infantryman shows the typical variations between shades of khaki and olive found in all the clothing and equipment of a vast army supplied from factories and depots dispersed over half a continent, along supply lines which were soon to be massively disrupted by enemy invasion. Note the characteristic raw-cut bottom edge of his greatcoat; and that, like many Red Army troops, he wears old-style ankle boots and puttees instead of calf-length *sapogi* boots.

This soldier still has the old M1930 "German"-style knapsack, which quickly became a rarity after 1941. Note the aluminium mug attached to the BN gasmask bag; during the war the gasmask was often discarded and its bag used as an all-purpose musette, since many soldiers never received packs. This man has a slightly different pattern of entrenching tool carrier from that shown in the photograph opposite. Strapped to his pack flap is the handsomely-shaped M1936 steel helmet, still in widespread use although a new and simplified pattern was introduced from 1940. The standard infantry weapon was the M1891/30 Mosin-Nagant 7.62mm bolt-action rifle, of elderly design.

Red Army Man, Rifle Forces, winter field dress, 1940

This rifleman is typical of the soldiers who endured such hardship during the mis-handled Winter War against Finland. He wears the 1936 *shlem* (or *budionovka,* so nicknamed after the Bolshevik cavalry hero of the Civil War, Semyon Budenny) with the crimson cloth star of his arm of service behind the metal Red Army badge. Note the greyer shade of his greatcoat - *shinel* - compared with those on pages 10 and 11; this was a common variation. His sheepskin mittens are pro-bably of local manufacture; and instead of high boots he wears laced ankle boots and puttees - inadequate in any winter conditions, and a guarantee of frostbite in a North Russian winter. An extra 70 rounds of 7.62mm rifle ammunition is carried in five-round charger clips in a canvas bandolier of Tsarist type. From the leather waist belt are suspended an aluminium water bottle in its olive drab cover, a canvas pouch for two F-1 hand grenades, and a single rigid leather rifle ammunition pouch of Tsarist pattern. The M1891/30 Mosin- Nagant had an old-fashioned cruciform socket bayonet, which was nearly always carried on the rifle - either fixed as here,or reversed when not in use.

Yefreitor of Tank Troops, field dress, 1939

By the outbreak of the Great Patriotic War the Red Army deployed the largest number of armoured fighting vehicles of any of the combatant nations - perhaps 28,000 in all. However, only a minority of this huge "paper" strength were actually serviceable, and a high proportion were of obsolescent types. Ironically, during the interwar years the Germans had circumvented the prohibitions imposed by the Treaty of Versailles with Soviet connivance (to their mutual benefit) by developing both tanks and aircraft on Soviet soil, and were thus well informed about Soviet capabilities when they launched Operation "Barbarossa" on 22 June 1941. By that winter only perhaps ten per cent of the pre-war Soviet tank strength were still functioning.

The uniform adopted for Soviet tank crews combined both French and German elements. The distinctive padded helmet was developed from the crash helmet worn by German pilots during World War I, whereas the leather coat came from France via the Tsarist army. The Tank Forces arm-of-service colour was black with scarlet piping, and the badge a yellow metal tank; note the collar patch worn here, in the same shape as that for the greatcoat, with the transverse bar of NCO rank. The gas-mask is the 1940 model.

Captain of Aviation, summer dress, 1939-40

The Air Force - *Voyenno Vozdushnye Sily* or V-VS - was an arm of the Red Army and not a separate service, so its personnel used the same rank titles and badges as the ground forces. In 1935 a distinctive new blue service uniform was introduced, consisting of a *shlem,* a *pilotka* cap (illustrated here), a peaked service cap, a greatcoat, a jacket, breeches and long trousers, all of dark blue with light blue piping. However, for economic reasons the blue uniform issue was discontinued with the outbreak of war; and thereafter officers often wore items of the blue and khaki uniforms concurrently. The arm-of-service colour was light blue, and the badge for flying personnel a winged propeller. Pilots and mechanics wore an embroidered badge on the upper left sleeve, as seen here.

The Captain's rank is identified by the single red-enamelled bar on his Air Force-blue collar patch, which bears the Air Force badge and is trimmed gold for an officer. The Air Force's light blue appears as piping and badge backing on his dark blue *pilotka* and seam piping on his semi-breeches. The lightweight khaki field blouse is of typical officer's cut, with a pointed end to the front placket and pleated pockets. On narrow cross-straps he wears a Tokarev semi-automatic pistol and a mapcase.

Captain of Aviation, 1939-40

The same officer dressed for colder conditions. The three-quarter-length leather coat of World War I inspiration was still common to a number of air forces in the 1930s, though the more cramped confines of the new generation of closed-cockpit aircraft would soon make it obsolete. It bears collar patches of the shape worn on greatcoats and "French" tunics, and the same left sleeve badge as the service and field uniforms. The dark blue Air Force *shlem* or *budionovka* cap, worn instead of the *pilotka* in cold weather, has the usual star-shaped cloth badge backing in arm-of-service colour. This headgear, and the belt with cross-strap, are of 1935 pattern.

Like the ground forces' tank fleet, a great majority of the military aircraft available in June 1941 were of obsolete types; and like the tanks, huge numbers of them were destroyed during the initial German advances, often while still on the ground. Like the tank force, too, however, the V-VS had already started to receive the first deliveries of the new equipment which would, in 1942, enable them to begin to strike back effectively.

Major-General of Rifle Forces, service dress, 1940-41

A divisional commander wearing a uniform of superior material and tailoring. The peaked cap bears the circular cockade introduced for general officers in 1940. The olive-coloured "French" is piped in scarlet, and the breeches have scarlet stripes in addition to the seam piping. On the 1935 pattern waist belt is the holster for the Korovine pistol. On the left breast is the "Order of Lenin" instituted in 1930, and the medal commemorating the "20th Jubilee of the Red Army of Workers and Peasants" established on 24 January 1938.

The outbreak of war caught the Rifle Forces in a state of partial reorganisation after the Winter War against Finland. Of the Red Army's 303 divisions 229 were Rifle, Mountain Rifle or Motorised Rifle formations. The April 1941 regulations gave a division about 14,500 men of three infantry and two artillery regiments, with weak anti-tank and anti-aircraft battalions and a light tank company. Over 100 Rifle Divisions were effectively destroyed in the summer 1941 fighting; all males between 23 and 36 years of age were immediately called up, and the formation of 286 new divisions was put in hand by the end of that year, though with establishments reduced to about 10,900 men.

Sergeant-Major of NKVD Frontier Troops, summer field dress, 1941

Although organised, trained and equipped along military lines the Frontier Troops came under the People's Committee of Internal Affairs (NKVD). These troops were a separate organisation from the NKVD's Internal Troops, which were primarily employed on internal security duties; at the outbreak of war NKVD troops totalled 15 Rifle and Cavalry Divisions, and were expanded rapidly thereafter (see also pages 44 and 50).

Many Frontier Troops detachments bore the full impact of Operation "Barbarossa", and distinguished themselves in combat, in the defence of Brest-Litovsk and elsewhere. The most distinctive feature of their uniform was the peaked cap, with bright green crown and dark blue band. Badges of rank were identical to those of the Red Army; this *starshina* has four enamelled triangles on collar patches with double red and gold edging and red central stripe. The submachine gun is an early example of the PPsH-41, at this date under trial and available only to picked troops. Its spare drum magazine, holding 71 rounds of short 7.62mm, was carried in the canvas pouch on the waist belt. He also has an aluminium canteen in a cloth carrier, a torch, and a slung binocular case and gasmask.

Lieutenant-General of Ground Forces, winter 1941-42

The tall cap - *papakha* - in grey astrakhan for general officers was introduced in 1940; it had a scarlet top decorated with a cross in gold lace, and the general officers' cockade badge pinned to the front. The scarlet-piped greatcoat is also the 1940 pattern, which was almost identical in general appearance to that worn during the Tsarist period. Note the two rows of six gilt metal buttons bearing the Soviet coat-of-arms; post-war coats have two rows of eight buttons. This gives a clear view of the general officers' sleeve chevron of rank - broad gold lace, with a narrow scarlet line at the bottom edge only. Note also the non-standard winter boots, of composite leather and felt construction.

The catastrophic losses of 1941 - perhaps a million dead and three million taken prisoner, representing more than half the USSR's total manpower losses over four years of war – led to the rapid promotion of many new, younger generals who learned the business of command under the most demanding conditions. Those who proved incapable often did not survive to be replaced; those who showed talent went on to lead the rebuilt and revitalised Red Army of 1943-45.

Lieutenant-Colonel of Artillery, field dress, 1941

This is more or less the standard field uniform for officers at the time of the German invasion. The *pilotka* had increasingly replaced the summer-weight *shlem/ budionovka* since the late 1930s, and although most officers seem still to have preferred the traditional peaked service cap the *pilotka* was a convenient field alternative to that headgear too. Note the fine quality of this officer's *gymnastiorka*, with scarlet piping on the collar and cuffs. New orders issued on 1 August 1941 abolished the rank chevrons on the forearms. This was followed on 3 August 1941 by an announcement that in future cap stars and buttons would be delivered in olive green finish, while those in use were to be painted. In practice, and particularly given the chaotic conditions of summer and autumn 1941, it would have been many months before such regulations were uniformly applied. The M1896 "broom-handle" Mauser semi-automatic in its wooden buttstock/holster was not standard issue, but was a popular private firearm among officers. The binoculars are the 1931 model.

Lieutenant-Colonel of Artillery, winter dress, 1941-42

The Lieutenant-Colonel wears here the winter service uniform with the new ear-flapped fleece cap - *shapka-ushanka* - introduced in 1940 to replace the winter weight *shlem/budionovka*. The officers' pattern was made of good quality grey astrakhan; that issued to the soldiers had synthetic pile, which they nicknamed "fish-fur". The 1935 pattern greatcoat still bears the sleeve rank insignia ordered removed in August 1941, which are still seen in many photographs dating from the mid- and late-war years. The coat is made from ordinary soldiers' material.

The Artillery was an arm of high prestige, and had long attracted ambitious and able officers. In 1941 Rifle Divisions had two regiments of 76mm, 122mm and 152mm guns and howitzers; the early massive losses in equipment cut this establishment to two battalions, one each of 76mm guns and 122mm howitzers, and infantry came to depend greatly on mortar fire support. As the war progressed, however, the Artillery was massively rebuilt, and became a decisive arm; the High Command Reserve forces, in which by 1945 about one-third of the total artillery assets were grouped, fielded entire Artillery Divisions and even Corps.

Junior Sergeant of Artillery, summer field dress, 1941-42

The steel helmet is the 1936 model, with a flared brim and a small applied comb or crest. It was issued in a grey paint finish, and often had an outline five-pointed star stencilled in crimson on the front. The *gymnastiorka* blouse and trousers are the standard issue; note the characteristic diamond-shaped reinforcements to the knees of the trousers. The full-colour collar patches were supposed to be replaced from April 1941 with subdued versions on plain khaki backing, but photographs show that they were often retained - indeed, occasional examples even survived the major uniform changes of 1943. The soldier wears non-elasticated puttees - which came in many colours, being made from all kinds of worn-out uniforms - and ankle boots; the familiar calf-length boots were far from universal, and several million pairs of laced shoes and boots were provided by the USA under Lend-Lease arrangements. The equipment comprises the M1938 pack, leather ammunition pouches for M1891/30 series weapons, a canvas pouch for two RGD-33 hand grenades, and the gasmask. The canvas sling over the left shoulder shows that he wears, obscured here, a water bottle of Tsarist pattern carried in a canvas pouch. The carbine is the M1891/38.

Political Officer of Artillery, field dress, 1941-42

Political officers were attached to the headquarters of all units: the *kommisar* to units of battalion size and greater, the junior grade or *politruk* to smaller sub-units. Commissars wore basically the same uniforms as line officers of the appropriate arm of service, but with different insignia. Their collar patches lacked the usual officers' gold trim (note that this commissar has the single rank bar marking his equivalence to a line Captain); and instead of the gold and red rank chevrons they wore on each forearm an embroidered red star badge with gold hammer and sickle (see page 58, fig.B).

This commissar wears a simple uniform *gymnastiorka*, without the piping often seen on officers' blouses. On the waist belt is a holster for the M1905 Nagant revolver. Note the compass worn strapped to the left wrist, as was the fashion at this time; and the usual binocular and map cases on leather cross-straps.

The system of joint unit command, shared between a line and a political officer, dated from the Civil War, when many unit commanders were former Tsarist officers whose loyalty was felt to require supervision. It was obviously a pernicious system, and many commissars, appointed for their Communist Party credentials rather than any military knowledge, interfered in military decisions with disastrous results. Their power was reduced in August 1940, but they had already done too much damage for the quality of unit command to recover quickly.

Trooper of Cavalry, 1941-42

The outbreak of war found the Red Army still with 13 cavalry divisions, even though the arm had been greatly reduced by the extensive mechanisation of the late 1930s; the Bolshevik cavalry had an honoured place in Civil War traditions, and in the affections of some senior commanders. In August 1941 the divisional establishment was reduced to 3,000 men - in effect, a brigade - but the number of divisions was increased, reaching 82 by the end of 1941. The cavalry's heyday was 1942, during the sweeping campaigns in the south; although tactically obsolete the mounted arm still had a real contribution to make under the special local conditions of the Russian Front, and fulfilled the mobile role with occasionally surprising success while the Red Army's mauled tank forces were rebuilt. Although later greatly reduced, the horsed cavalry arm still had formations at the front in 1945.

Cavalrymen were issued with the same basic uniform as the rest of the Red Army, but photographs show that many retained the old-style blue breeches and peaked service cap as field dress surprisingly late in the war. This arm of service was identified by blue and black, which appear here on the cap and collar patches, the latter bearing the badge of crossed swords on a horseshoe. The sabre is the Tsarist model originally introduced in 1881 but manufactured again under the designation M1927. The leather supporting straps with a pocket for a whistle were usually reserved for officers. The carbine is the M1891/38.

Junior Lieutenant of Tank Troops, field dress, 1941-42

The expensive black leather coat of the pre-war period was replaced by one made of black canvas, in a slightly different cut; it is worn here with the usual "greatcoat-shape" collar patches in the black and scarlet arm colours, with the single red-enamelled brass square of this rank. In 1935 officers of the Tank Troops, like those of the Air Force, received a prestigious new service dress consisting of peaked cap, *pilotka*, jacket, breeches and long trousers; for tank officers these were in steel grey. The peaked cap, illustrated here, had a black velvet band and scarlet piping, while the jacket had scarlet piping on the collar and cuffs and was worn with shirt and tie. The same insignia were worn on the jacket as on the blouse. In the field elements of this uniform would be worn with the khaki *gymnastiorka;* as the war progressed often only the steel grey cap would be retained with standard khaki field uniforms.

The massive pre-war mechanised forces comprised some 29 Corps, each with one Motor Rifle and two Tank Divisions. The primary equipment was still the T-26 infantry tank and BT series cavalry tanks, roughly comparable to the German PzKpfw II which they still faced in considerable numbers, though outclassed by the PzKpfw III. Serviceability was very poor, however; more than 40 per cent of the total inventory was seriously unserviceable, spares were in short supply, and in the summer 1941 battles huge numbers of Soviet AFVs were abandoned broken down, apart from the thousands destroyed in action by the more experienced and better-led Panzerwaffe.

Motorcyclist of Tank Troops, field dress, 1941-42

The steel helmet is the 1936 model, on which are worn typical goggles of the period. The black canvas coat is of the pattern issued to the crews of some armoured fighting vehicles, worn here with gauntlets and lightweight summer boots by a motorcyclist of the reconnaissance and communications element attached to a Tank Brigade. The sub-machine gun is the PPsH-41.

The devastating losses suffered by the mechanised forces in summer 1941, despite local successes achieved by some units which had already received the excellent T-34 tank, led to a rapid reorganisation. Mechanised Corps were abolished from mid-July 1941, and most surviving Tank Divisions were disbanded. The available tanks and crews were re-assigned to much smaller units, more in keeping with the available levels of replacements (and of command competence). These Tank Brigades were the equivalent of Western tank battalions, with a "paper" strength of 93 tanks (though some had as few as 15), plus a Motor Rifle company. The reorganisation coincided with the epic uprooting of much of the remaining industrial capacity from European Russia to beyond the Urals; and the single factory then turning out the T-34 - the Stalingrad Tractor Works - performed miracles of energy and improvisation. In the battles before Moscow in October-December 1941 the tank, and several of the new Brigades equipped with it, proved themselves the equal of the best the Wehrmacht could throw at them.

25

Civil Defence Woman, 1941-42

In pre-war Soviet Russia civil defence and pre-military training was undertaken by the voluntary Society for Aviation and Chemical Preparation *(Osoaviakhim)*. At the beginning of the war civil defence became the responsibility of an organisation called *Protivo-Vozduchnya-Oborona* (PVO). As the Wehrmacht struck ever deeper into Russia, Byelorussia and the Ukraine the civil populations of towns and cities were mobilised on a massive scale. Often after a long day's work in war factories, perhaps on very low food rations, women of all ages turned out in their thousands to perform every kind of duty that would free the men for service at the front, from digging vast systems of anti-tank ditches with pick and shovel to serving as fire-watchers during nightly enemy air raids.

This girl air raid warden's outfit consists of a version of the British steel helmet made by a Leningrad saucepan factory, an army shirt with *Osoaviakhim* and Voluntary Medical Society badges on the left breast, and a civilian skirt. She carries tongs for the handling of blazing incendiary bombs, which she is expected to simply pick up and drop in a bucket of water.

Kuban Cossack, winter field dress, 1941-42

Because of their privileged status in pre-revolutionary Russia, the Cossacks had provided the White armies of the Civil War with some of their fiercest troops; and under Communist rule they paid a terrible price. It was only with caution that Cossack units were introduced into the Red Army, at least in name, in 1936; and the number of true Cossacks recruited into these five retitled Cavalry Divisions is questionable. However, each of the three main Cossack "hosts" or *voiska* for which the new divisions were named received its own distinguishing elements of uniform.

Don Cossacks had a tall black fleece cap or *papakha* with a scarlet top, while Kuban and Terek Cossacks both wore the lower *kubanka*, with scarlet and blue tops respectively, with crosses of braid or tape. In wartime all wore standard Red Army field uniform with cavalry distinctions, and certain traditional additions. Round his neck this trooper wears the cold weather hood or *bashlyk* , and on his shoulders the stiff black *burka* cape. The PPsH-41 sub-machine gun was widely issued to cavalry, being handy for horseback use; note also the M1927 dragoon sabre, a not uncommon wartime alternative to the Cossack *shashka* sabre.

Engineer Second Class, field dress, 1941-42

Officers of certain technical and administative branches wore collar patch rank insignia of the same type as equivalent line officers, but without the gold patch edging or forearm rank chevrons. Here the peaked cap and collar patches bear the arm-of-service colours of black with blue piping, and a crossed hammer and spanner badge is worn on the collar patch. The equipment is the 1932 pattern for mounted officers with two supporting straps.

Junior Sergeant of Engineers, field dress, 1941-42

He wears standard summer-issue uniform of the Red Army with the *pilotka* (which by 1942 had almost entirely replaced the summer-weight *shlem* as field headgear for the rank and file), blouse and breeches all made from olive green cotton drill. The collar patches are black with blue piping and the crossed hammer and spanner badge; the rank badge is a red enamel triangle. From his leather waist belt he carries an entrenching tool in its pouch, a bayonet for the SVT-40 semi-automatic rifle, and a pair of wire cutters. In his right hand he carries a wooden tool box and in the left a kerosene lamp.

Senior Sergeant of Tank Troops, field dress, 1941-42

During the war the leather tank helmet was replaced by one made of black or grey canvas. It was also issued in a fleece-lined version for winter use. Over the standard field uniform crews of armoured vehicles normally wore an overall, officially in black but often in grey or khaki as a result of dispersed manufacture - some were even made in Canada under Lend-Lease - which was usually worn without insignia. The holster, made from synthetic leather, was for the Tokarev TT-30 semi-automatic pistol.

Lieutenant of Tank Troops, 1941

Tank officers, like their comrades in the Aviation branch, often wore items of their grey service dress together with standard issue khaki clothing. This officer wears an issue blouse with officer's badges of rank, which despite the order of August 1941 have not yet been modified. On his left breast he wears the first version of the "20th Jubilee of the Red Army" medal; later this medal was worn with a grey ribbon with a red stripe along each edge.

Red Army Man, Motor Rifles, winter field dress, 1941-42

This soldier is typical of the troops from Siberia who threw the Germans back from the gates of Moscow in December 1941; and those who carried the war to the enemy during the following winter, finally winning a decisive victory in the encirclement of Stalingrad. The Motor Rifles, despite their designation, were seriously short of motorised transport, and instead employed the hazardous method known as *tankoviy desant* - riding the T-34 tanks themselves into battle and only disembarking to fight on foot at the last moment.

The snow camouflage suit, cut either as here in a loose smock and overtrousers, or with a greatcoat - length upper garment, was worn over the basic field uniform and special winter clothing. This comprised a padded (*telogreika*) or sheepskin jacket, padded trousers (*vatnie sharovari*), a *shapka-ushanka* fleece cap, and sometimes *valenki*, a type of compressed felt boot for very cold temperatures - a prized version of these had a waterproof rubberised lower section. Here the pre-war leather belt has been replaced by one of wartime manufacture which combines webbing and synthetic leather. The pouch contains a spare drum magazine for the PPsH-41; these sub-machine guns were lavishly issued to the Motor Rifles as the war progressed – 57, and 27 rifles, per company, instead of the normal infantry ratio of 12 to 85 – plus nine DP light machine guns.

Leading Seaman of the Red Fleet, 1941-42

At the outbreak of war the Navy represented less than six per cent of the total manpower of the armed forces (contrasting with the Ground Forces with 79 per cent and the Air Force with 11.5 per cent). Much of the Red Fleet was bottled up in harbour for most of the war, naval operations being largely limited to coastal surface and submarine operations in the Baltic and Black Seas and direct support of land operations on these seaboards. In addition to the Naval Infantry brigades which already existed in 1941, many other Navy personnel were formed into ground combat units. Land-based sailors were prominent in the defence of Leningrad during the epic siege, and in the Crimea in 1942.

On the sleeves of the reefer jacket or *bushlat* this Leading Seaman *(starshy krasnoflotets)* wears his badge of rank: a five-pointed red star outlined yellow. His seaman's cap bears a tally identifying the "Northern Fleet". He wears bell-bottom trousers over standard issue army boots; the traditional blue and white striped cotton undershirt was also worn by Naval Infantry, often with standard issue Red Army khaki uniform. His equipment includes a fabric Maxim machine-gun belt worn as a rifle ammunition bandolier, as traditionally carried by sailors serving on land (who were not normally issued with ammunition pouches, although this sailor has acquired one); the waist belt supports two RGD-33 grenades, and a personal sheath knife. The rifle is the M1891/30 Mosin- Nagant with bayonet fixed.

Major-General of Artillery, field dress, 1943

The service cap is of the simplified field issue widely worn by all officer ranks from the mid-war years, all in khaki without arm-coloured band or piping, though it retains the general officers' cockade cap badge. Just visible is the piped standing collar of the newly introduced 1943 *kitel* tunic of Tsarist cut. Over it the 1940 model generals' greatcoat is worn; piping was scarlet for combatant arms of service, crimson for technical arms and light blue for Aviation. The new insignia prescribed by the regulations of 15 January 1943 have been applied to the coat. On parade greatcoats the collar patches - of the shape illustrated, and plain apart from gold edging and buttons - were scarlet for Marshals, scarlet or black for Generals of combatant arms, crimson for technical arms and light blue for Aviation. On field greatcoats all collar patches were khaki with gold edging. The buttons for general officers bore the Soviet coat-of-arms; note that they are painted khaki-green for field use.

For all ranks insignia of branch and exact rank moved from collar patches - which were no longer worn on everyday uniform tunics and blouses - to the newly reintroduced and traditionally shaped shoulder boards. These came in service and field qualities; for officer ranks the former incorporated metallic lace and the latter were of khaki material. This Major-General has field shoulder boards of figured khaki material, piped red round the edges, and bearing the single silver star of this rank.

Pilot of Red Army Aviation, winter flying suit, 1940-43

This pilot wears cold weather flying gear typical of that seen in Finland during the Winter War of 1939-40 and in Russia during the early part of the Great Patriotic War. The canvas suit and the leather flying helmet are lined with fleece, and are worn with lined boots and heavy fur gauntlets. While this kind of clothing was very necessary in many of the obsolescent types still in service in 1941 - some were even open-cockpit biplanes - less cumbersome gear, including a more advanced flying helmet, was issued to the pilots of the closed-cockpit single-seat fighters - Lavochkins, MiGs and Yakovlevs - which became available in greater numbers from 1942. There were no special rank badges for wear on flying clothing. The pistol was carried either in a holster as shown, or in a special pocket inside the flying overall or jacket.

Sergeant-Major of Rifle Forces, winter field dress, 1943

A classic image of the Red Army infantryman at Stalingrad in winter 1942-43, and throughout the second half of the war. The *shapka-ushanka* synthetic pile winter cap is the model introduced in 1940, and bears the universal enamelled Red Army badge on the front flap. The January 1943 field shoulder boards, of khaki cloth piped in the crimson-red of the infantry and bearing the yellow T-shaped braid ranking of the *starshina,* have been attached here (as was normal only for senior NCOs and officers, rather than the rank and file) to the khaki padded jacket or *telogreika* which had become common issue by the end of 1943 even in central and southern zones; it appeared in various slightly different versions, some with a fall collar. Matching padded trousers were often issued, but this soldier wears it with the standard khaki wool semi-breeches with reinforced knees. Note that he wears the medal "For Service in Action", which was awarded over five million times: it was common for Red Army men to wear medals on combat clothing. Although he is armed with the now ubiquitous PPsH-41 (whose 71-round magazine and short range encouraged aggressive offensive tactics), he also carries the bayonet for the SVT-40 Tokarev semi-automatic rifle as an all-purpose blade. In addition he carries an F-1 fragmentation grenade, and an entrenching tool - the latter perhaps sharpened for use as a hand-to-hand weapon, as in the World War I trenches.

Major of Artillery, winter field dress, 1943

This officer wears the *shapka-ushanka* of higher quality, made of real lambswool. His greatcoat, however, is made from coarse brownish-grey issue material like those of the soldiers. It bears field collar patches, and field shoulder boards made from khaki cloth with red piping and rank stripes (see pages 59 to 61 for close-up photographs of the rank sequence of shoulder boards, in service and field versions). Under the greatcoat can be seen the two-button standing collar of the revised January 1943 pattern *gymnastiorka*; buttons bore the five-pointed star and hammer and sickle emblem. The holster is for the M1895 Nagant 7.62mm revolver, obsolete but still issued to some officers, NCOs, machine gunners, signallers, drivers, etc. The fieldglasses are the 1931 model.

Red Army Man, Rifle Forces, 1943

Another classic image of the Red Army infantryman of the second half of the war. The M1940 helmet was painted olive green, some pre-war examples having the stencilled outline red star. The enlisted men's 1943 blouse has a standing collar, no breast pockets, and detachable field shoulder boards. He wears on the right breast the badge of "Distinguished Rifleman", and on the left the medal for the "Defence of Stalingrad" established on 22 December 1942. The difference in shade between garments is not significant; dispersed manufacture led to a wide range of drab khakis, collectively referred to as *zashchitniy tsvet*. On the web belt are the water-bottle, pouches for F-1 grenades and the PPsH-41 drum magazine. On his back he has a simple cotton knapsack, *veshchevoi myeshok* - a bag with drawstring throat and fabric straps.

(Left)

Lieutenant-Colonel of Rifle Forces, 1943

The khaki service cap has a crimson band and piping, and the blouse cuffs are also piped in infantry colour. The 1943 blouse has internally hung breast pockets, and field shoulder boards of arm and rank. This regimental commander still wears the blue, piped breeches, though khaki would have been as common. The officers' equipment is the pattern introduced in 1943 with a two-prong frame belt buckle; he has a mapcase, a holstered Tokarev, and a flare pistol.

(Above)

Sergeant, Medical Service, field dress, 1943

The standard 1943-pattern field uniform of olive drab *pilotka,* blouse and semi-breeches - here, superior examples with cuff and leg piping in Rifles crimson rather than Medical dark green; under front line conditions he would wear what he could get. Over these he wears the olive cotton duck ground sheet - *plashch-palatka* - arranged as a poncho.

Orderly, Medical Service, 1943

Many of the medical personnel serving at the front, often even under fire, were women. The dark blue beret and skirt were official service and parade uniform for Red Army women personnel dating from pre-war days, and were retained under regulations of May and August 1942. For duty in the field khaki equivalents were prescribed, but under front line conditions most women seem to have been issued standard male uniform, or to have worn whatever mixed outfits were convenient. The arm-of-service colour for medical personnel was green with scarlet piping and the arm-of-service emblem a serpent and chalice. This orderly carries the standard issue medical musette bag.

Under the pressure of casualties women were accepted first into non-combat support branches, and later into combat arms. They served as anti-aircraft gunners; as snipers, though apparently not in the ranks of line Rifles units; and as combat aircrew, in three famous all-woman regiments. In the last year of the war qualified women from tank factories were recruited as combat tank drivers, some rising to command positions. There were 76 awards to women of the ultimate decoration,"Hero of the Soviet Union", many of them posthumous; of the total, 27 went to aircrew, 12 to medical personnel, ten to snipers and scouts, and one to a member of the Tank Forces.

Partisan "Uncle Kapa", 1943

The rapid German advances of 1941 and 1942, through a vast and often sparsely inhabited landscape rich in concealing forests and swamps, naturally left huge numbers of disorganised Red Army stragglers in their wake. Although many were captured, tens of thousands avoided this fate (tantamount to a death sentence, given German treatment of Soviet prisoners of war). Many of these, marooned deep in German-held territory, continued to wage war – often to considerable effect. The Wehrmacht was forced to commit very large numbers of troops to security duty in the rear areas, where partisan bands recruited both from soldiers and from local civilians preyed constantly upon their lines of communication. The NKVD established contact with many of the larger groups, and actively sponsored and supplied them whenever feasible. Despite the most ruthless methods the Germans never succeeded in stamping out major partisan activity.

Partisans used whatever clothing and weapons they could get, combining items of Soviet and German military issue with civilian clothes. From his waist belt, which is fastened by a German buckle modified with a cut-out star, this partisan has hung a German Mauser Kar.98k bayonet, a Russian M1914/30 hand grenade and a "Molotov cocktail". His main weapon is a captured, and much-prized, 9mm German MP.40, for which he also has the canvas triple magazine pouches. He is eating from a can of American corned beef, which prior to the Allied landings in Normandy was known ironically as the "Second Front".

Major of Rifle Forces, service dress, 1943-44

The 1943 *kitel* officer's tunic was usually worn with "everyday" - i.e. service dress - shoulder boards faced with gold or silver metallic lace, rather than the field service pattern as here; but under the circumstances of total war such trivialities as exact conformity with uniform regulations did not come high in the order of priorities. The service cap has the Rifles' crimson band piping, while the *kitel* has scarlet piping on the collar and cuffs; as for the greatcoat, the sequence of combat arm-of-service colours was simplified here to either scarlet or (for Tanks and Artillery) black. Note the five-button front and internally hung breast pockets with external flaps. The blue breeches have crimson piping.

Major-General of Ground Forces, 1943-44

The 1943 regulations naturally took some time to apply, and composite uniform and insignia combinations were quite common throughout the war. This divisional commander still wears a blouse with the 1935 pattern falling collar, but has removed the pre-1943 collar patches and attached 1943 regulation shoulder boards. These are of field service pattern, which for general officers were made from khaki lace in a zig-zag weave with hand-embroidered silver stars according to rank. The plain khaki cloth field service cap - which was widely worn by all officer ranks in the second half of the war - has a khaki cloth-covered peak and khaki cloth strap in place of black patent leather. This type of cap was nicknamed the "Kirov" after the old Bolshevik leader. The khaki field service breeches appeared in both piped and plain versions. This particular pattern of mapcase was supplied under Lend-Lease.

(Far left)
Major of Tank Forces, 1944

Serving in the Tank Regiment of a Motor Rifle Brigade, he wears a combination of Rifles and Tank clothing. The rubberised coat, padded tank helmet (in brown leather or grey or black canvas), goggles and gauntlets were all items issued to AFV crews. He has added field shoulder boards and greatcoat-style collar patches in red-piped khaki. The holster has the extended attachments intended primarily for tank officers.

(Left)
Lieutenant-Colonel, NKVD, 1944

The most distinctive feature of NKVD troops was the peaked cap with blue top, brick red band and crimson piping. The 1943 blouse differs from the Army version in having pleated patch breast pockets, and blue cuff piping. The shoulder boards had blue stripes and backing. NKVD troops used the appropriate arm-of-service badges in silvered metal; NKVD security personnel wore none.

(Right)
Major of the Medical Service, 1944

Doctors and Veterinarians were identified by dark green cap bands and scarlet piping. Their shoulder boards were narrow, only 4.5cm compared with the 6.5cm of line officers; they had silver lace and scarlet stripes and backing. The grey officer's raincoat, to which everyday shoulder boards and greatcoat-style collar patches are here attached, does not seem to have been widely available.

Camouflage Clothing

A number of different suits of loose camouflage overgarments were produced during the war, and issued mainly to snipers, to scouts - *razvedchiki* - including engineer scouts and some armoured reconnaissance units, and to mountain troops. These were made in both one- and two-piece versions, cut very generously so that they could be worn over any combination of uniforms and equipment, and with large hoods which could be closed over the steel helmet.

(**Above left**) The most common camouflage clothing in wartime photographs, this was characterised by a large, well dispersed, "rounded jigsaw" camouflage pattern. This is a two-piece example; there were also one-piece coveralls. Colours seem to have varied; apart from this brown on tan type, the suit also appeared with black or alternatively dark green patterning on a pale olive drab background. Note the

very large hood, fastening well down over the shoulders and chest – a characteristic of all Red Army camouflage overgarments.

(**Above second left**) The simplest form of camouflage: garlands of olive green artifical grass (rafia) were produced, for wrapping round the body, equipment, and weapons to break up their visual outline.

(**Above second right**) Later in the war an alternative type of suit was produced - though never in the same quantities - termed the *mochalniy*. This was in olive green, cut similarly to the "jigsaw" pattern suits, but with many small cotton loops all over the surface to which tufts of rafia grass were knotted: wear and tear over the years have reduced the tufts on this example to stubs, and they would originally have been much larger. Obviously, field-expedient foliage was also attached at need, to blend the colours in with the locally dominant seasonal growth.

(**Above right**) The type of long-cut snow smock issued to ski troops during the Winter War against Finland in 1939-40, and much more widely during the Great Patriotic War.

Some photographs show a reversible winter coverall, made of olive material with a pattern of white blotches on one side only; it is not clear when this was introduced or how widely it was issued.

(Right) Red Army Scout, 1944-45

This is the final pattern of camouflage suit to be introduced during the Great Patriotic War, which first made its appearance in 1944, and does not seem to have been very widely issued before the final victory over Germany. Note the complexity of the pattern: over a pale tan background are printed a sparse pattern of the old brown "rounded jigsaw" blotches, and overall a tightly interlinked, saw-toothed "seaweed"-shaped pattern of a medium and a dark green.

The sub-machine gun is the 7.62mm PPS-43, the lighter and cheaper successor to the PPsH-41, which to a limited extent began to replace the latter during the last two years of the war. Born of the PPS-42, which was designed and produced by an engineer named Sudarev inside besieged Leningrad and tested in action straight from the factory bench, it was made as simple as possible; it had a folding skeleton butt, fired only on full automatic, lacked the chromed chamber and bore of the PPsH-41, and took a 35-round box magazine which was much handier and simpler than the complex clockwork-operated 71-round drum. Three spare magazines are carried in a simple canvas pouch with the flap secured by cord loops and wooden toggles. The sheath knife is the 1940 model, although most surviving examples seem to bear the date 1943. The helmet is the M1940; the laced ankle boots could be Soviet, Lend-Lease or captured German types.

Junior Lieutenant of Rifle Forces, winter field dress, 1944

The sheepskin coat was a popular item of winter clothing, which was both issued and privately acquired; known as the *shuba* or *polushubok,* depending on length, it was used by both infantry and mechanised personnel. Note the fastening, by cloth extension tabs and buttons on the right side of the chest; a slash pocket, hidden here by the mapcase, was let into each side below the waist. Shoulder boards were the only insignia worn on this coat. The officer's personal equipment is as previously described.

Captain, NKVD Frontier Troops, parade dress, 1945

The officer's *mundir* parade tunic (made in both single- and double-breasted versions - here the latter) had a waist seam, skirts, and rear skirt pocket flaps. It was introduced in 1943, but did not make its appearance until the June 1945 Victory Parade in Moscow. The Frontier Troops' version illustrated differed from that of the other troops of the NKVD only in the green colour of the piping and the backing for the lace collar and cuff patches. On his breast this officer wears the "Order of the Red Banner", instituted on 1 August 1924; and the medals "For Service in Action" and "Victory over Germany".

(Left)

Senior Lieutenant of Aviation, service dress, 1945

On the V-VS officer's peaked cap the badges were hand-embroidered and the cockade was gilt metal with a light blue enamel centre. The light blue arm-of-service piping appeared on the cap, the collar and cuffs of the *kitel* and on the breeches (and the trousers worn with walking-out uniform). The medal is for the "Defence of Moscow", which was established on 1 May 1944.

Lieutenant-Colonel of the NKVD, summer service dress, 1945

The white cap cover and unpiped white cotton *kitel* were worn by officers with everyday and undress uniforms in summer. The shoulder boards are blue with gold lace; the other NKVD distinguishing colour, brick red, appears on the cap band. This internal security officer wears no arm-of-service badge on his shoulder boards. Breeches piping was officially brick red prior to February 1943, blue thereafter, but in practice both would be seen in use in 1943-45.

NKVD security troops did see some front-line combat, but were more usually deployed as "blocking detachments" in the rear to prevent the line troops retreating. They were employed in the repression and mass deportation of ethnic groups suspected of being disloyal to the regime, both during and after the war, and in prolonged operations against anti-Soviet partisans in the Ukraine and the Baltic republics which lasted into the early 1950s. With some 50 divisions their strength was equal to about ten per cent of the total man-power of Red Army Rifle divisions in 1945.

Lieutenant of Naval Aviation, parade dress, 1945

Although the USSR had no aircraft carriers, the Naval Aviation arm was active during the war from coastal bases, particularly in the Baltic theatre in 1944-45 when retreating German forces used sea transport.

The naval parade uniform was introduced at the end of the war and was worn at the June 1945 Victory Parade. It preserved the essential distinctions of previous naval uniforms. Whereas line officers had gold lace and buttons, members of the technical branches had silver. In the Naval Aviation arm the piping on the cuffs was light blue, and the shoulder boards had silver lace and light blue stripes and backing; no arm-of-service badge was worn on the shoulder boards. The parade dagger or *kortik* is the model introduced in 1940.

Lieutenant-General of Rifle Forces, parade dress, 1945

This is the new "wave green" parade uniform worn by Marshals and Generals, commanders of Fronts and Armies, who paraded in Moscow on 21 June 1945 to celebrate the victory over Germany. Orders were worn on the right breast of the double-breasted *mundir,* and medals on a bar or *kolodka* on the left. The sabre is the 1940 pattern.

(Right)
Junior Sergeant of Rifle Forces, parade dress, 1945

The Victory Parade was headed by a contingent carrying German Imperial and Wehrmacht colours which had been captured in Berlin. They were trooped by infantrymen wearing the enlisted ranks' "everyday" or service uniform introduced in 1943 but not generally issued until the end of the war. The tunic, termed a *mundir*, had a standing collar, pocket flaps in the rear skirts, and scarlet piping on the collar, cuffs and rear pocket flaps. The collar here bears patches of Rifles crimson with, for this rank, a longitudinal line of yellow lace; the shoulder boards are in the Rifles' crimson with black piping, with the Junior Sergeant's two yellow lace bars. On the right breast are the Orders of the "Red Star" and "Patriotic War", above the "Guards" badge marking a unit awarded the Guards title for distinguished combat service. On the left breast is the gold star of a "Hero of the Soviet Union", above a *kolodka* of service and campaign medals. He slights the colour of a German Army infantry battalion.

Helmets and Personal Equipment

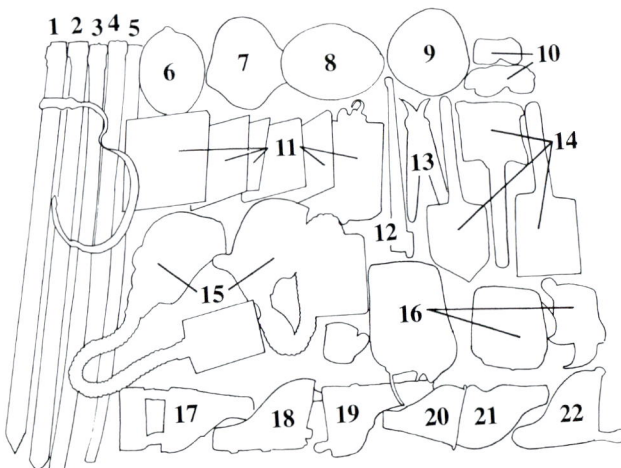

(1) Officers' belt Models 1932 and 1943
(2) Officers' belt Model 1935
(3) Soldiers' leather belt
(4) Sergeant-Majors' leather belt
(5) Soldiers' webbing and synthetic leather belt
(6) M1916 "Adrian" steel helmet
(7) M1936 steel helmet
(8) M1938 Civil Defence steel helmet
(9) M1940 steel helmet
(10) Goggles (two patterns)
(11) Map cases (six patterns)
(12) M1891/30 bayonet in canvas scabbard (rarely seen)
(13) Wire cutters
(14) Entrenching tools and carriers (three patterns)
(15) Gasmasks and filters (two patterns)
(16) Binoculars and cases (three patterns)
(17) Holster for Tokarev TT-33 pistol for crews of armoured vehicles
(18) Holster for Tokarev pistol in synthetic leather
(19) Holster for M1903 Browning pistol
(20) Holster for Korovine pistol
(21),
(22) Holsters for M1895 Nagant revolver

Weapons and Pouches

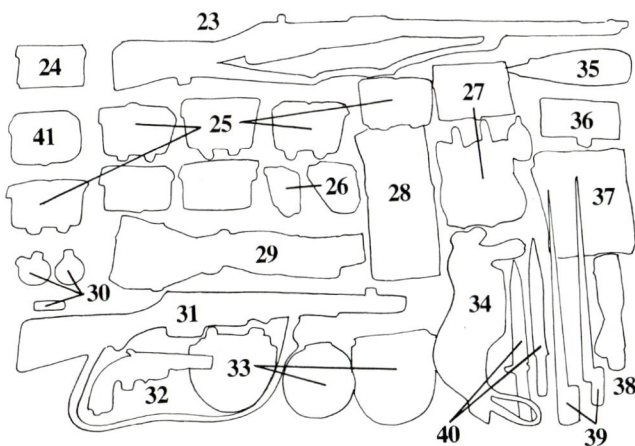

(23) M1891/30 Mosin-Nagant rifle and webbing sling

(24) Pouch for M1891/30 rifle ammunition, Tsarist pattern

(25) Pouches for M1891/30 rifle ammunition, Soviet pattern

(26) Pouches for Mannlicher rifle ammunition

(27) Pouches for F-1 grenades

(28) Pouch for RGD-33 grenades

(29) Bandolier for M1891/30 rifle ammunition

(30) Tin oil bottles, and five-round charger clip, for M1891/30 rifle

(31) PPsH-41 sub-machine gun

(32) Flare signal pistol

(33) Drum magazine for PPsH-41, flanked by two patterns of pouch

(34) M1896 Mauser pistol in wooden holster-stock

(35) Improvised incendiary grenade ("Molotov cocktail")

(36) M1944 synthetic leather pouches for M1891/30 rifle ammunition

(37) Magazine pouches for PPS-43 sub-machine gun

(38) M1914/30 hand grenade

(39) Bayonets for M1891/30 rifle

(40) Bayonet for SVT-40 rifle

(41) Pouches for SVT-40 rifle ammunition

55

(Right) A selection of Red Army soldiers' small personal necessities and belongings, including water bottles; torches; cooking and eating utensils; toilet articles; cigarette packets and cases, matches and lighters, etc. At bottom right, note three examples of German military belt buckles adapted for wear by Soviet soldiers.

(Below) A selection of wartime orders, medals and badges, typical training manuals and personal documents and photographs from the early war period.

INSIGNIA

Collar Patches

(A) Major, Tank Troops, field blouse and tunic, 1935 pattern

(B) Field officer, Rifles, parade tunic, 1943 pattern

(C) Private First Class, Rifles, greatcoat, 1935 pattern

(D) Marshal of the Soviet Union, all uniforms, 1935 pattern

(E) Senior Lieutenant, Frontier Troops, field blouse and tunic, 1935 pattern. Frontier post personnel did not wear gold officers' patch edging.

(F) General officers, greatcoat, 1943 pattern

(Mollo Collection, photograph Michael Dyer Associates)

A

B

C

D

E

F

Cloth Insignia

(A) Forearm rank chevron, Junior Lieutenant, 1935 pattern
(B) Forearm badge for Political Officers
(C) Left sleeve badge, Air Force pilot, khaki field uniform
(D) Left sleeve badge, Air Force pilot, blue "everyday" service uniform
(E) Left sleeve badge, Military Traffic Regulator
(F) Left sleeve badge, Anti-Tank Artillery personnel

Shoulder Boards, 1943 Pattern
(All are of "everyday" service uniform quality unless otherwise indicated)

(A) Private, Rifles, field uniform
(B) Yefreitor (Private First Class), Air Force
(C) Junior Sergeant, Artillery
(D) Sergeant, Technical Troops
(E) Senior Sergeant, Artillery, field uniform
(F) Sergeant-Major, Tank Troops

(Mollo Collection, photographs Michael Dyer Associates)

Shoulder Boards, 1943 Pattern

(A) Officer Cadet (Junker), Artillery Technical Branch

(B) Junior Lieutenant, Air Force, field uniform

(C) Lieutenant, Tank Regiment within Motor Rifles formation

(D) Senior Lieutenant, Legal branch, field uniform.(This width of shoulder board was also worn by Medical and Veterinary officers.)

(E) Captain, Signals, field uniform

(F) Major, Artillery Technical Branch

(A) Lieutenant-Colonel, Tank Troops
(B) Colonel, Air Force (Austrian manufacture)
(C) Major-General, field uniform
(D) Lieutenant-General, field uniform
(E) Colonel-General, Technical Branches
(F) General of the Army, field uniform

(Mollo Collection, photographs Michael Dyer Associates)

A   B   C

D   E   F

Para-Military Breast Badges

(A) Voroshilov Marksman of the Red Army, 2nd Category; instituted 1934

(B) "Ready for the Medical Defence of the USSR"; instituted 1934

(C) "Ready for Anti-Aircraft and Anti-Chemical Defence", Osoaviakhim, 2nd Category; instituted 1936

(D) Voroshilov Marksman of Osoaviakhim, second type; 1933 pattern

(E) Voroshilov Horseman of Osoaviakhim; instituted 1936

(F) Voroshilov Horseman of Osoaviakhim, 2nd Category; instituted 1939

(G) Sports Parachute Instructor of Osoaviakhim (& Red Army); instituted 1933

(H) "Ready for Work and Defence of the USSR"; instituted 1931

A   B   C

D   E   F

G   H

Military Breast Badges

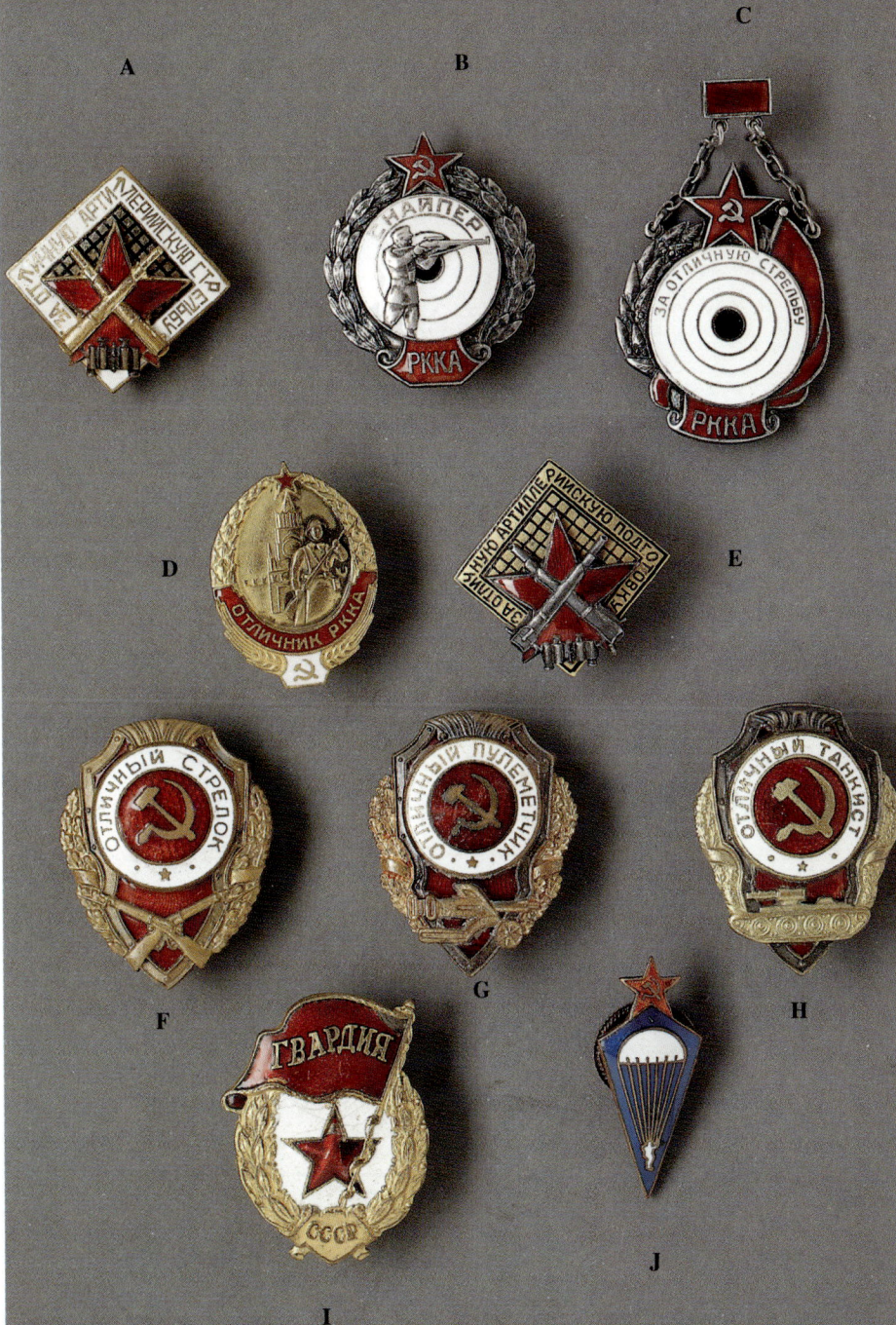

(A) Distinguished Marksman of the Red Army; instituted 1938

(B) Sniper of the Red Army; instituted 1938

(C) Distinguished Gunlayer of the Red Army; instituted 1936

(D) Distinguished Soldier of the Red Army; instituted 1939

(E) Distinguished Artillery Preparation of the Red Army: instituted 1936

(F) Distinguished Rifleman; instituted 1942

(G) Distinguished Machine Gunner; instituted 1942

(H) Distinguished Tankist; instituted 1942

(I) Guards personnel; instituted 1942

(J) Parachutist (originally Sports Parachutist of Osoaviakhim); instituted 1936

(Mollo Collection, photogaphs Michael Dyer Associates)